◇ ◇ ◇ ◇

10 Rules to Beat Laziness:
A Journey to Living Fully

◇ ◇ ◇ ◇

A book by Chris Y.H.

CHAPTERS

Introduction: The Truth About Laziness   2

Rule 1: Define Your Purpose   5

Rule 2: Set Achievable Goals   11

Rule 3: Master Your Mindset   18

Rule 4: Build Momentum with Small Wins   28

Rule 5: Overcome Procrastination   33

Rule 6: Optimize Your Environment   40

Rule 7: Energy Management   45

Rule 8: Accountability and Support Systems   50

Rule 9: Embrace Discipline Over Motivation   55

Rule 10: Reward Yourself and Celebrate Progress   60

Conclusion: Living Fully   65

◊ ◊ ◊ ◊

Introduction:

The Truth About Laziness

◊ ◊ ◊ ◊

Introduction: The Truth About Laziness

Laziness. It's a word we've all heard, perhaps even labelled ourselves with at some point. But what does it really mean? Society often equates laziness with a lack of ambition or effort, yet the truth is far more nuanced. Laziness is rarely about being idle; it's often a symptom of something deeper—fear, overwhelm, or even a lack of clarity about what truly matters.

"Laziness is nothing more than the habit of resting before you get tired," quipped Jules Renard, highlighting the irony of our tendency to avoid action even when it's in our best interest. But what if laziness wasn't an inherent flaw? What if it were a challenge we could overcome to unlock a more meaningful and productive life?

In this book, we'll explore the strategies and tools that can help you beat laziness and, in doing so, take a step closer to living fully. As the Roman philosopher Seneca once said, "It is not that we have a short time to live, but that we waste a lot of it." This is your opportunity to reclaim that wasted time.

Why Laziness Matters

The consequences of unchecked laziness go beyond missed deadlines or unfulfilled potential. Laziness erodes self-esteem, damages relationships, and can even lead to long-term unhappiness. Yet, it's important to approach this issue with compassion. Beating laziness isn't about pushing yourself to the brink or adopting a hyper-productive mindset. It's about finding balance and building habits that align with your goals and values.

Take a moment to consider this: How many times have you wanted to start something new—a project, a workout routine, a business idea—only to feel paralyzed by the effort required? You're not alone. Laziness thrives in the gap between intention and action, and this book is your guide to bridging that gap.

The Journey Ahead

In the chapters that follow, we'll break down the 10 rules to overcome laziness. These aren't abstract concepts or empty platitudes; they are actionable steps grounded in psychology, neuroscience, and real-world examples. From mastering your mindset to building momentum with small wins, each rule is designed to equip you with the tools to take control of your life.

You'll learn to identify and overcome the root causes of laziness, whether it's fear of failure, perfectionism, or simply a lack of energy. You'll discover the power of small, consistent actions and how they can snowball into significant change. And most importantly, you'll redefine your relationship with effort and discipline, seeing them not as burdens but as pathways to a richer, more fulfilling existence.

A Personal Reflection

I didn't write this book because I've always been the epitome of productivity. In fact, it's quite the opposite. There were times in my life when laziness held me back, and I felt trapped in a cycle of procrastination and regret. It was only through trial and error—and a lot of self-compassion—that I discovered the principles I'm sharing with you now.

This journey isn't about perfection; it's about progress. It's about waking up each day and choosing, however imperfectly, to take one step forward. As you embark on this journey, remember that change doesn't happen overnight. But with patience and persistence, it does happen.

A Call to Action

As you read this book, I encourage you to actively engage with its lessons. Take notes, complete the exercises, and most importantly, apply what you learn. The real transformation happens not in reading but in doing. Think of this book as a roadmap. The destination? A life where laziness no longer stands in the way of your potential.

So, are you ready to beat laziness and start living fully? Let's turn the page and begin this journey together!

◊ ◊ ◊ ◊

Chapter 1:
Rule 1 – Define Your Purpose

◊ ◊ ◊ ◊

Chapter 1: Rule 1 – Define Your Purpose

Overcoming laziness begins with a simple yet profound realization: the importance of defining your "why" i.e., your purpose. Without a clear sense of direction, it's easy to feel stuck, unmotivated, and lost. You might find yourself procrastinating, struggling to take action on things that are important, and feeling a sense of stagnation, even though you know there's more to life. But once you define your purpose—once you understand the deeper reason behind what drives you—the fog lifts, and motivation flows naturally. When your actions are linked to something meaningful, the smallest task becomes an opportunity for growth, and even the biggest obstacles become stepping stones to a greater goal.

Living with a defined purpose does more than just help you fight laziness—it gives your life a sense of meaning and direction. The energy that once felt drained can be replenished, and the sense of exhaustion and stagnation can be replaced with enthusiasm and clarity. The first step toward overcoming procrastination is establishing a strong internal foundation—a purpose that resonates deeply with who you are and what you want to achieve.

The Power of Purpose

Purpose is not just a motivational concept; it's a fundamental aspect of what makes us resilient in the face of challenges. It serves as the internal compass that guides us through life, helping us make decisions, maintain focus during hard times, and stay driven even when everything around us seems chaotic. When you're clear on your purpose, you can withstand life's uncertainties with a sense of peace because you know that each action you take is connected to something far greater than mere tasks or short-term goals.

As Friedrich Nietzsche once said, "He who has a reason to live can bear almost any how." This insight emphasizes the resilience that a clear purpose offers. When your life is driven by purpose, external circumstances and setbacks lose their power to derail you. You can weather storms because the destination is clear, and the journey becomes one of meaning, even if the road is rocky.

However, this connection to purpose isn't always easy to maintain. Life can sometimes throw us off course, and external influences can make it difficult to stay aligned with our true desires. The people we surround ourselves with, our work environments, and even societal expectations can cause us to lose sight of what's truly important to us. It's common for individuals to feel pressured to meet others' expectations or adopt paths that aren't in alignment with their own purpose, simply because those paths seem easier or more acceptable in the short term.

The Struggle with External Influences

External factors can play a significant role in steering us away from our deeper motivations. Society often places immense pressure on individuals to conform to certain standards of success, which may not align with one's personal desires or values. From a young age, we are taught what we should aspire to—whether it's a specific career, a type of lifestyle, or a certain definition of success. These external pressures can be so pervasive that they overshadow our true desires, leading us to pursue goals that we never truly chose for ourselves.

For example, many individuals find themselves working in careers that don't spark passion, simply because they were told that success meant climbing the corporate ladder or obtaining a prestigious title. The result is a feeling of emptiness and dissatisfaction, even when outwardly, things seem to be going well. When we become too focused on the expectations of others, we often lose sight of what brings us joy, fulfilment, and motivation.

Family dynamics can also influence our decisions and purpose. We might feel obligated to pursue certain paths to please our parents, peers, or loved ones, even if they don't align with what we truly want for ourselves. For instance, if your parents have always envisioned you becoming a doctor, you might feel guilty about pursuing a career in the arts, even though it's where your true passion lies. The desire to meet others' expectations can be a strong force, and it often leads us to compromise on our own goals, leaving us feeling disconnected from our true purpose.

Peer pressure can be just as powerful. In a world dominated by social media and external validation, it's easy to become caught up in the image of what others are doing, comparing your progress to theirs. The constant exposure to other people's successes or lifestyles can create feelings of inadequacy and push you to follow trends or chase goals that are not aligned with your authentic self. Over time, this external noise can drown out your inner voice, making it harder to distinguish between what you truly want and what others expect from you.

Life experiences, too, can cloud our vision. Setbacks, failures, and disappointments can make us question whether we're on the right path or if our aspirations are even worth pursuing. After facing challenges, it's easy to become discouraged and lose sight of our larger vision. The pain of past mistakes or regrets can become a powerful distraction, tempting us to stay small or to avoid setting new goals out of fear of failure.

The Importance of Returning to Your Core

Despite these challenges, it is crucial to reconnect with your core beliefs and desires. Moving away from your true purpose is natural at times, but the important thing is to recognize when it's happening and take action to realign yourself with what truly matters. The process of re-discovering your deeper motivations is ongoing. Your goals, values, and sense of purpose will continue to evolve as you grow, and that's okay. What matters is that you stay committed to the pursuit of what is meaningful to you, regardless of external pressures.

To help you stay aligned with your purpose, regular self-reflection is key. Spend time regularly evaluating whether your current actions, goals, and relationships align with your deepest desires. Are you living the life you truly want, or are you following someone else's idea of success? Reflecting on these questions can help you course-correct if necessary.

One of the best ways to reconnect with your purpose is to pause and take a step back. In a world that demands constant productivity and achievement, we often forget to slow down and listen to ourselves. Create space in your life for quiet moments of introspection. Disconnect from the distractions and noise, whether that's social media, work pressures, or external judgments, and tune in to your inner self. Ask yourself: What do I really want? What feels true to me? When you carve out time to reflect and be honest with yourself, you allow your purpose to rise to the surface once again.

Practical Tools for Staying Aligned

Once you've defined your purpose and are aware of the influences that may pull you off track, it's essential to implement practical strategies to keep yourself aligned with your true goals.

1. Set Boundaries:

It's essential to protect your energy and time from people or situations that pull you away from your purpose. While relationships are important, it's necessary to set boundaries with people who may unintentionally undermine your goals. This could mean limiting time with individuals who have a negative impact on your mindset or who don't understand or support your aspirations.

2. Practice Mindfulness:

Mindfulness is the practice of being present in the moment and paying attention to your thoughts, feelings, and surroundings without judgment. By cultivating mindfulness, you can better recognize when external influences are starting to distract you from your purpose. Mindfulness helps you regain control over your actions, ensuring that you make decisions based on your own desires rather than external pressures.

3. Create a Vision Board or Journal:

Visual tools such as vision boards or journals can serve as reminders of your long-term goals and aspirations. Place images, quotes, or affirmations on your board that reflect your deepest desires and revisit it regularly. Writing in a journal can also help you process your emotions, track your progress, and reconnect with your purpose when distractions arise.

4. Surround Yourself with Supportive People:

While some relationships can pull you off course, others can keep you grounded in your purpose. Surround yourself with people who uplift you, support your dreams, and encourage you to stay true to yourself. Seek out mentors, friends, or accountability partners who share similar values and who will challenge you to grow in a positive direction.

Overcoming Setbacks and Staying Motivated

Even when you are clear on your purpose, there will still be challenges and setbacks that make it difficult to stay on course. It's important to remember that setbacks do not define your journey—they are part of the process. The key is to stay resilient and remember that your purpose remains unchanged, even when external circumstances seem to shift.

One of the most powerful ways to remain motivated is to focus on small, incremental steps. When life feels overwhelming, break your goals down into manageable chunks. Celebrate each milestone, no matter how small, and use those moments of success as fuel to keep going. Every effort, no matter how insignificant it may seem at the time, is a step toward a greater purpose.

Closing Thoughts

The path to overcoming laziness and living a fulfilling life begins with understanding what truly drives you. Your purpose is the foundation upon which you build your actions, decisions, and goals. It gives you the strength to endure challenges, the motivation to keep moving forward, and the clarity to make decisions that align with your deepest values. Life will always present obstacles, distractions, and pressures from the outside world, but your purpose can serve as an anchor—helping you stay grounded, focused, and resilient in the face of external influences.

By defining your purpose and committing to it, you set the stage for a life that is full of meaning, intention, and fulfilment. As you continue to grow and evolve, your purpose will guide you, inspire you, and remind you of the incredible potential you have to create the life you truly desire. Embrace it and watch as it transforms your life.

◊ ◊ ◊ ◊

Chapter 2:

Rule 2 – Set Achievable Goals

◊ ◊ ◊ ◊

Chapter 2: Rule 2 – Set Achievable Goals

Setting achievable goals is one of the most powerful ways to overcome laziness and ignite lasting motivation. Without clear goals, it's easy to feel lost or overwhelmed, unsure of where to start or how to move forward. But when you break down your larger ambitions into smaller, manageable actions, you create a roadmap to success—one that keeps you motivated, focused, and consistently moving forward. The key lies in understanding the art of setting goals that not only challenge you but also push you toward consistent progress.

Think of your life as a journey, and goals as the landmarks along the way. Without these markers, it's easy to drift without direction, waiting for inspiration to strike or a shift in circumstance to push you into action. But this passive approach often leads to frustration and stagnation. Instead, setting achievable goals gives you the control to steer your life with purpose, ensuring that every day is an opportunity to take meaningful steps toward a future you've intentionally crafted.

The Power of SMART Goals

A proven method to create clear and effective goals is the SMART framework, a powerful tool that empowers you to break down even the most ambitious dreams into bite-sized, actionable steps. SMART goals are:

Specific: The more clearly you define your goal, the more likely you are to achieve it. Vague goals like "I want to get fit" or "I want to save money" can leave you feeling uncertain about where to begin. A specific goal, on the other hand, clearly defines exactly what you want to achieve.

Measurable: Progress is motivation. If you cannot measure how far you've come, it's easy to lose sight of your progress or feel that you're not advancing at all. Including measurable elements in your goals lets you track progress and celebrate small wins along the way.

Achievable: It's essential to ensure that the goal you set is realistic. While it's important to push yourself, goals that are too far out of reach can create unnecessary stress and demotivate you before you even begin. Achievable goals are those that challenge you within the context of your current resources, skills, and constraints.

Relevant: Your goal must align with your broader purpose or aspirations. It's easy to set goals that sound good on paper or seem logical, but they should resonate with your deeper values and long-term ambitions. A goal that is relevant to you personally fuels intrinsic motivation, making it more meaningful and worthwhile.

Time-bound: Finally, setting a deadline helps create a sense of urgency. Without a time frame, procrastination creeps in, and you lose momentum. Having a specific end date for your goal encourages you to stay focused, make decisions faster, and build discipline.

Let's see how applying these principles works in practice.

Instead of saying, "I want to exercise more," a **SMART** goal would be:

> "I will jog for 20 minutes three times a week for the next month."

This goal is **specific** (jogging), **measurable** (20 minutes, three times a week), **achievable** (a realistic commitment based on time and energy), **relevant** (it contributes to better health), and **time-bound** (one month).

Here's another example:

Replace "I'll save money" with…

> "I will save $500 by setting aside $50 per week for the next 10 weeks."

This goal is **specific, measurable, achievable, relevant** (saving money for a specific purpose), and **time-bound.**

Instead of saying "I'll improve my skills," try:

> "I will complete an online course on graphic design within six weeks by dedicating 5 hours per week."

Again, the goal is **specific, measurable, achievable, relevant,** and **time-bound**. This structure doesn't just give you clarity on what needs to be done — it provides a roadmap to follow and a way to measure success.

Breaking Big Tasks into Manageable Steps

One of the most common reasons people procrastinate is the overwhelming feeling that comes with facing a big goal. When you think of a task as a massive, undifferentiated whole, it's easy to freeze up, unsure of where to begin. But breaking a large goal into smaller, manageable steps allows you to create momentum, enabling you to take consistent action with minimal stress.

The first step in breaking down big tasks is to start with the end goal. Imagine the final outcome you want to achieve. For example, if your goal is to publish a blog post, the final outcome is clear—you want to have a post live on your website for readers to see. However, the path to achieving that goal requires more than just "writing a post." There are many milestones along the way.

The next step is to identify those major milestones. For a blog post, this could include:

- Researching topics
- Drafting an outline
- Writing the content
- Editing and proofreading the post
- Publishing the post
- Promoting the post

Once you've broken your goal into these key phases, it's time to create actionable tasks for each milestone. For example, when researching, you could set a task like "spend 2 hours gathering ideas from reputable sources." When it comes to drafting, set a specific task such as "write the introduction and main points in a single sitting." Each of these smaller tasks is easy to start and checking them off one by one creates a sense of accomplishment that drives you forward.

Once you've broken down the larger milestones into actionable tasks, prioritize the tasks. Start with the ones that will make the biggest impact or provide the necessary foundation for other tasks. For instance, researching should come before drafting, because you'll need to gather your ideas before you start writing.

Setting deadlines for each of these smaller tasks is crucial for keeping you on track. Deadlines keep you accountable, create a sense of urgency, and help prevent procrastination. Without deadlines, it's easy to lose focus and allow the task to drift indefinitely.

Tools for Goal Tracking

Tracking your progress is an essential part of staying motivated. Without regular monitoring, it's easy to lose sight of how far you've come or how much work remains. Fortunately, there are many tools available to help you stay organized, manage your goals, and track your progress in real-time.

Goal-Tracking Apps:

Apps like Trello, Notion, or Asana allow you to visually organize tasks and create boards or lists for different projects. They make it easy to break down your goals into smaller steps and provide a space to mark off completed tasks. You can also set reminders for deadlines, making sure you never miss an important step. Additionally, these apps allow you to reflect on your progress, which is essential for maintaining momentum.

Journals:

Whether you prefer a handwritten journal or a digital one, maintaining a record of your goals, tasks, and achievements can be an incredibly powerful tool. A journal serves as a place for self-reflection and personal accountability. You can use it to jot down daily or weekly goals, track progress, and adjust your plans if necessary. Writing things down also solidifies your intentions and allows you to gain clarity on your purpose and goals.

Habit-Tracking Apps:

If consistency is a challenge, habit-tracking apps like Streaks or Habitica can help you build and maintain positive habits. These apps use gamification to reward you for staying consistent with your goals, making the process of goal completion more fun and engaging. Habitica, for example, turns your goals into a role-playing game where you can earn points and rewards for completing tasks. This can make staying on track feel less like work and more like an adventure or a challenging game.

Practical Exercises to Get Started

If you're ready to take action and start setting achievable goals, here are some practical exercises to help you get started.

Daily Goals Worksheet:

Each day, write down 3-5 specific goals you want to accomplish. These should be small, actionable steps that you can easily track and complete. For example, "Write 500 words for my blog post," or "Spend 30 minutes researching a new topic for my business." As you complete each task, check it off. This simple process provides a sense of accomplishment and keeps you moving forward.

Weekly Planning Session:

Dedicate 20 minutes each Sunday to plan your upcoming week. Reflect on what you accomplished the previous week, identify areas for improvement, and set goals for the week ahead. Use this time to ensure that your goals align with your long-term aspirations and that each task is achievable within the given time frame.

Progress Reflection:

At the end of each week, take some time to review your progress. Reflect on what worked, what didn't, and what lessons you learned along the way. Adjust your goals if necessary and celebrate the milestones you've reached. This practice not only helps you track your progress, but it also reinforces the connection between effort and reward.

Overcoming Challenges and Building Momentum

It's inevitable—there will be days when you face obstacles, lack motivation, or feel like giving up. But remember that the key to success isn't perfection; it's persistence. Stay focused on your next actionable step and remind yourself that progress, no matter how small, is still progress. Every task completed, every goal reached, no matter how minor it may seem, is a victory.

In times of difficulty, return to your original purpose. Why did you set these goals in the first place? What motivates you to keep going, even when things get tough? When you stay focused on the bigger picture and celebrate small wins along the way, the journey becomes less about the end goal and more about the progress you're making toward something greater.

Closing Thoughts

The process of setting achievable goals is not just about accomplishing tasks—it's about creating a roadmap that guides you toward success. By making your goals specific, measurable, achievable, relevant, and time-bound, you lay the foundation for consistent progress. Breaking down big tasks into manageable steps reduces overwhelm and builds momentum. With the right tools and strategies, you can stay organized, track your progress, and remain motivated, even when challenges arise. Remember, success is not an overnight achievement—it's built, step by step, one goal at a time. Stay committed, take action, and watch as your dreams begin to take shape.

◊ ◊ ◊ ◊

Chapter 3:

Rule 3: Master Your Mindset

◊ ◊ ◊ ◊

Chapter 3: Rule 3 – Master Your Mindset

The mind is a powerful thing. It shapes your reality, influences your emotions, and governs the decisions you make every single day. But here's the catch: too often, we let our mind work against us. We become victims of our thoughts—our fears, doubts, and insecurities controlling our actions, or worse, paralyzing us into inaction. When we are stuck in this cycle, it's easy to fall into laziness. We feel overwhelmed, discouraged, and trapped in the belief that we are not capable of achieving the things we dream about.

But here's the truth: your mindset is not fixed. It's malleable. And the power to shift it lies within you. When you take control of your mindset and cultivate the right frame of mind, everything changes. You gain the strength to face challenges head-on, the resilience to push through setbacks, and the motivation to take consistent action toward your goals. You break free from the chains of laziness and step into the life you are truly capable of living.

This chapter is all about learning to master your mindset—understanding how your thoughts shape your behaviour, overcoming the self-doubt that holds you back, and adopting strategies to cultivate a mindset that supports growth, progress, and success.

How Mindset Influences Behaviour

Your mindset is more than just a collection of thoughts—it is the lens through which you see the world. It influences how you interpret your experiences, how you react to obstacles, and how you perceive your potential. In other words, your mindset dictates your behaviour. If your mindset is one of defeat, that will show in your actions. If your mindset is one of possibility, that will show in your actions as well.

To understand how mindset shapes behaviour, let's look at two types of mindsets: the fixed mindset and the growth mindset.

The Fixed Mindset vs. The Growth Mindset

A person with a fixed mindset believes that their abilities, intelligence, and potential are set in stone. They believe they are either "good" at something or "bad" at it, and this belief influences how they approach challenges. If they encounter something difficult, they might quit because they believe they are not capable of overcoming it. The fixed mindset is rooted in fear of failure, because failure is seen as a confirmation of their lack of ability.

On the other hand, a person with a growth mindset believes that abilities and intelligence can be developed through effort, learning, and persistence. They see challenges as opportunities to grow and learn. When faced with a setback or failure, they do not view it as a reflection of their worth or ability. Instead, they see it as a lesson—a step along the journey of improvement.

The mindset you adopt profoundly affects your behaviour. If you have a growth mindset, you are more likely to take action, even when you feel unsure or when the path forward is unclear. You are not paralyzed by fear; you move forward with curiosity and determination. In contrast, if you have a fixed mindset, you might find yourself procrastinating, avoiding difficult tasks, or convincing yourself that you're not capable of succeeding, which ultimately leads to laziness.

The good news is that you can change your mindset. You don't have to stay trapped in limiting beliefs. By cultivating a growth mindset, you can unlock the doors to success and fulfilment and begin to take consistent action toward your goals.

Overcoming Negative Self-Talk and Excuses

One of the most significant obstacles to mastering your mindset is the negative self-talk and excuses that arise whenever you are faced with discomfort or doubt. These inner voices are incredibly convincing, often making us believe that we are not good enough, that we don't deserve success, or that the task ahead of us is too difficult. We've all been there. You wake up in the morning, and before you even get out of bed, your mind starts running through a list of excuses:

"I'm too tired to work out today."

"I don't have time for that."

"I'll start tomorrow."

"This is too hard; I'll never be able to do it."

"I'm not cut out for this."

... and the list goes on.

These excuses are just that—excuses. They are not truths. And yet, they hold so much power over us. The more we listen to them, the more they grow. The more we give in to them, the more they dictate our behaviour, keeping us stuck in a cycle of laziness and inaction.

The key to overcoming negative self-talk is to become aware of it. You must become the observer of your thoughts. When those excuses pop up, don't simply accept them as reality. Challenge them. Ask yourself, "Is this thought helping me move closer to my goals, or is it holding me back?" Most of the time, you'll find that the excuses are not rooted in truth—they're based on fear, doubt, or the desire to avoid discomfort.

One powerful way to combat negative self-talk is to replace it with positive affirmations. Affirmations are positive, present-tense statements that help reprogram your subconscious mind. When you repeat affirmations, you are not just stating a belief; you are shifting your internal dialogue and planting the seeds of new, empowering thoughts. For example, instead of thinking, "I'll never be able to finish this project," replace that with, "I am capable of completing this project and I will take the next step today." The more you repeat affirmations like this, the more you will believe them. Over time, these new beliefs will become your truth.

Another powerful technique to combat negative self-talk is self-compassion. Rather than berating yourself for feeling lazy or unmotivated, treat yourself with kindness and understanding. Understand that it's okay to struggle, and that overcoming laziness doesn't happen overnight. Be patient with yourself and focus on progress, not perfection. Every small step you take toward your goal is a victory.

Strategies for Cultivating a Growth Mindset

Adopting a growth mindset is essential to overcoming laziness and stepping into your full potential. A growth mindset is the belief that your abilities and intelligence can be developed through hard work, persistence, and learning. It's the realization that you are capable of growth and improvement, no matter where you are starting from.

Here are some strategies for cultivating a growth mindset:

1. Embrace Challenges

People with a growth mindset actively seek out challenges because they see them as opportunities for growth. They understand that the more difficult a task is, the more they will learn from it. Instead of shying away from difficult situations, they lean into them, embracing the discomfort as part of the process.

When you start to embrace challenges, you will find that the things you once thought were hard are now manageable. The feeling of accomplishment you get from overcoming a challenge builds momentum and strengthens your belief in your abilities.

2. Learn from Criticism

Feedback, whether positive or negative, is a valuable tool for growth. Those with a growth mindset welcome constructive criticism because they see it as an opportunity to learn and improve. They don't take feedback personally; instead, they ask themselves, "What can I learn from this?"

Criticism is not a reflection of your worth; it's simply information that can help you grow. Instead of letting criticism fuel self-doubt, use it to fuel your progress.

3. Celebrate Effort, Not Just Results

In a fixed mindset, people often focus solely on the end result. They tie their self-worth to their successes, believing that they are only worthy if they achieve a certain goal. But in a growth mindset, effort is just as important as the outcome. When you focus on the process and celebrate the effort you put in, you create a sense of satisfaction that is not dependent on external outcomes.

If you spend hours working on a task, even if the result isn't perfect, take pride in the effort you put forth. Celebrate your dedication and persistence and use that energy to propel you forward to the next step.

4. Cultivate Curiosity and Learning

People with a growth mindset have an innate curiosity about the world around them. They believe that they can always learn something new, no matter their age or experience level. Cultivate this curiosity in yourself. Commit to lifelong learning, whether that means reading a book, taking a course, or simply engaging in conversations with others who have different perspectives.

The more you expose yourself to new ideas and experiences, the more you'll discover about yourself and your potential.

5. Be Persistent!

A growth mindset requires persistence. When faced with failure, people with a growth mindset don't give up; they try again, and again, and again. They see failure as a part of the process, not a roadblock.

If you're struggling with laziness or procrastination, the key is to keep moving forward, no matter how small the steps may be. Don't let setbacks discourage you. Instead, see them as lessons, and use them to fuel your determination to keep going.

Actionable Tips: Affirmations, Visualizations, and Gratitude Practices

Mastering your mindset requires consistent effort and practical tools that can help shift your thoughts, beliefs, and behaviours. The right strategies allow you to replace negativity and procrastination with positive action and a more empowering view of your capabilities. Here, we'll dive deeper into key practices that will help you harness the power of your mindset in a way that drives meaningful change.

1. Daily Affirmations

Affirmations are a powerful tool to influence your internal dialogue. The thoughts we think shape the reality we experience, and affirmations act as a way to reprogram the subconscious mind to believe in our ability to succeed. Many people struggle with negative thought patterns and self-doubt, especially when faced with challenges. By consistently affirming positive beliefs about yourself, you can replace these limiting thoughts with empowering ones that propel you into action.

The key to effective affirmations lies in repetition and emotional connection. Repeating affirmations alone won't have the desired effect unless you truly feel them and believe them. When you say, "I am capable of achieving my goals," allow yourself to visualize the success you are striving toward. Connect with the feeling of achievement and allow that energy to motivate you.

Here are a few examples of affirmations that can help you overcome laziness and develop a growth mindset:

"I have the power to create the life I want."

"Every day, I am growing, improving, and becoming more resilient."

"I embrace challenges because they help me grow."

"I trust in my ability to learn from every experience."

"I take action consistently, no matter how small the step."

To make your affirmations even more powerful, write them down in a journal at the start of your day. This physical act engages your mind and body, helping to reinforce the belief. You can also record your affirmations in your voice and listen to them during the day, creating a more immersive experience.

2. Visualization

Visualization is another potent tool that can boost your mindset and motivate you to overcome laziness. This technique involves mentally rehearsing your success by vividly imagining yourself achieving your goals. When you visualize success, you are not only creating a mental image of the end result, but you are also emotionally attaching yourself to that success. This connection increases your motivation and builds the belief that what you want to achieve is possible.

To make visualization even more effective, follow these steps:

Find a Quiet Space:

Take a few moments to sit comfortably without distractions. Close your eyes and take a few deep breaths to calm your mind.

Visualize in Detail:

Picture the goal you want to achieve. Visualize the process in as much detail as possible. For example, if your goal is to complete a project at work, imagine yourself working on it step by step. Feel the satisfaction of making progress. Picture the positive feedback from others when you finish it.

Embody the Emotion:

As you visualize, tap into the emotions you would feel if you achieved your goal. Do you feel pride, relief, joy, or excitement? These emotions are crucial, as they create a stronger mental connection to your desired outcome. The more vivid the emotion, the more likely you are to be motivated to take real-world action.

Make It a Routine:

To make visualization a habit, do it at the same time each day, such as in the morning before you start work, or before bed as you unwind. Just five to ten minutes of focused visualization can have a huge impact on your motivation.

The power of visualization lies in its ability to activate the same neural pathways that are triggered when you actually perform the task. Over time, this prepares your brain to take the necessary actions to achieve your goals.

3. Gratitude Practice

Gratitude is one of the simplest yet most powerful ways to shift your mindset. When you focus on what you're grateful for, you train your mind to see abundance rather than scarcity. Gratitude fosters a sense of positivity and contentment, which can drive you to take action toward your goals rather than procrastinating out of fear, overwhelm, or dissatisfaction.

The practice of gratitude works because it helps you reframe negative thoughts. When you feel down or lazy, practicing gratitude shifts your focus from what's wrong to what's right in your life. This simple change in perspective can increase your sense of motivation and help you overcome the inertia of laziness.

Here's how to start a daily gratitude practice:

Start Small:

Begin by writing down three things you are grateful for each day. They don't have to be big things. For instance, you might be grateful for a hot cup of coffee, a conversation with a friend, or a quiet moment in the morning.

Be Specific:

The more specific you are about what you are grateful for, the more meaningful the practice becomes. Instead of just saying "I'm grateful for my family," try "I'm grateful for the way my partner always listens to me when I'm feeling stressed."

Feel the Gratitude:

Don't just write down the words—feel the gratitude in your heart. The emotional connection is what activates the benefits of this practice.

End the Day with Gratitude:

Before going to bed, reflect on the positive moments of the day. What went well? What did you achieve? Focusing on the good things in your life, no matter how small, helps you end the day on a positive note, creating a sense of accomplishment and contentment.

You can also take it a step further by keeping a gratitude journal, where you reflect on your gratitude daily and track your mindset over time. This allows you to see patterns in your thinking and helps you notice how the practice of gratitude transforms your outlook.

4. Mindfulness and Meditation

Mindfulness and meditation can significantly enhance your ability to master your mindset. These practices help you stay present and focused, which is crucial when it comes to overcoming procrastination. Mindfulness allows you to become more aware of negative thought patterns as they arise, giving you the power to interrupt them before they take hold. Meditation, on the other hand, cultivates a sense of inner peace and clarity, allowing you to approach challenges with a calm and focused mind.

If you are new to meditation, consider using guided meditation apps like Headspace or Calm. These apps offer short, structured sessions that can help you develop a daily meditation habit and improve your focus, mindfulness, and mindset. A very important tip for incorporating mindfulness into daily life is that you don't need to sit in silence for hours to practice mindfulness. You can incorporate it into your everyday activities. Whether you're washing dishes, walking to work, or eating lunch, bring your full attention to the task at hand. This increases your ability to stay focused and reduces distractions, making it easier to take productive action.

5. Setting Micro-Goals

Sometimes, the thought of tackling a big goal can feel overwhelming. It can lead to procrastination or laziness because the task ahead feels too large or intimidating. One way to overcome this is by breaking your goals down into micro-goals. Micro-goals are small, specific tasks that take only a few minutes to accomplish but are aligned with your larger objectives. Setting micro-goals allows you to gain momentum, experience quick wins, and build confidence. When you successfully complete a small task, it reinforces your belief that you are capable of achieving bigger things. This sense of accomplishment fuels your motivation and drives you to take on more challenges.

Closing Thoughts

Mastering your mindset is one of the most important steps in overcoming laziness. Your mindset influences everything—your thoughts, your behaviour, and your results. When you adopt a growth mindset, practice self-compassion, and challenge negative self-talk, you open the door to a world of possibility. Remember, it's not about being perfect—it's about taking consistent action, embracing challenges, and learning from every experience. Your mindset is the key to unlocking your potential, so start today. Transform your thoughts, master your mindset, and watch as your life begins to change; slowly but surely.

◊ ◊ ◊ ◊

Chapter 4:

Rule 4: Build Momentum with Small Wins

◊ ◊ ◊ ◊

Chapter 4: Rule 4 – Build Momentum with Small Wins

Momentum is one of the most powerful forces in the world. It's the energy that propels us forward, helping us break free from the paralysis of laziness and begin moving toward our goals. Yet, the trick isn't always in having grand plans or sweeping actions. Often, the most effective way to overcome inertia and make progress is by starting small, accumulating small wins, and gradually building up to greater success. This is the essence of momentum—the simple idea that success begets more success.

The Science of Habit Formation

Before we can truly understand how small wins can build momentum, it's important to take a moment to explore the science behind habit formation. At the core of every successful endeavour lies consistency. While most people know that to overcome laziness and achieve their goals, they must take consistent action, the secret lies in how we create consistency in the first place.

Habits are automatic behaviours that are formed over time, often without conscious thought. They are the result of repeated actions that become ingrained in our neural pathways. The process of habit formation follows a simple loop: cue, routine, reward. A cue triggers the behaviour, the routine is the action taken, and the reward is the positive outcome or feeling we experience as a result of completing the action. This loop becomes stronger as we repeat it, turning once intentional actions into automatic behaviours.

The first time you set out to accomplish something, it feels like a struggle. You have to think about every step and actively remind yourself to stay on track. However, with repetition, the actions become easier, and the brain no longer requires as much mental energy to engage in them. Eventually, what once required conscious effort becomes second nature, and you don't have to push yourself as hard to get started. This is where small wins come into play.

When we begin with small, manageable actions, the brain experiences success more frequently. These little victories trigger the reward system in the brain, releasing dopamine and creating a positive feedback loop. Each success, no matter how small, reinforces the desire to keep going. Small wins activate the part of the brain responsible for motivation, making it easier to take the next step, and the next, until momentum is fully established.

How to Start Small and Build Consistency

One of the biggest reasons people struggle with overcoming laziness is that they view their goals as overwhelming. The sheer size of the task often paralyzes them before they even begin. The idea of writing a book, losing weight, or launching a business may seem too far off, too difficult, or too time-consuming. This overwhelming feeling causes procrastination and stasis. What people fail to realize is that you don't need to accomplish everything all at once. The key is to break down the task into bite-sized, manageable pieces that make it easier to get started and create momentum.

Think about the process of learning to walk. You didn't go from sitting to running; you first had to master the art of crawling, then standing, then taking a few steps before walking became second nature. Over time, the more you practiced and the more wins you had—no matter how small—the easier it became. This same principle applies to any goal you set for yourself. It's about starting small, building confidence, and then gradually increasing the challenge as you develop the skill and discipline to handle more.

To build momentum with small wins, the first step is to identify a manageable task within your larger goal. Let's say your long-term goal is to exercise more regularly. Instead of committing to an hour at the gym every day, start with something smaller and easier to achieve. You could commit to just 10 minutes of stretching or a 5-minute walk around the block. While this may seem trivial, the act of doing it—especially on days when you're feeling unmotivated—creates a sense of accomplishment. The small win reinforces the belief that you can succeed and that taking action, no matter how small, leads to progress. Over time, as your consistency builds, you can gradually increase the duration and intensity of your workouts, without feeling overwhelmed or discouraged.

Building momentum through small wins works because it shifts your focus away from the end goal and places it on the process. Instead of feeling discouraged by the distance between where you are and where you want to be, you begin to value each incremental step as a sign of progress. Every time you achieve a small win, you reinforce the belief that success is within reach. This creates a positive cycle that makes the larger goal feel more attainable, even if it's still a long way off.

It's also important to celebrate those small wins. Too often, people overlook the significance of these incremental achievements, believing that only major accomplishments matter. However, taking a moment to acknowledge and celebrate the little victories along the way is crucial. It reinforces the progress you've made, boosts your morale, and propels you forward with even more energy and enthusiasm.

Real-Life Examples of Using Small Wins to Overcome Inertia

The power of small wins is not just theoretical—it's something that has been proven time and time again in real life. People have achieved remarkable success by starting small, building momentum, and gradually increasing the scope of their efforts. Let's look at some real-life examples of how individuals have used small wins to break free from inertia and laziness. The names of these people, of course, are pseudonyms.

1. Sarah's Weight Loss Journey

Sarah had always struggled with her weight. She'd tried countless diets and exercise programs, only to lose motivation after a few weeks. The thought of losing 50 pounds felt overwhelming, and as soon as she slipped up or missed a workout, she felt defeated. But Sarah decided to change her approach. Instead of focusing on the large goal of losing weight, she started with small, manageable actions. She began by committing to a 10-minute walk every day after dinner. At first, it felt insignificant, but over time, that small win became a powerful habit. After a few weeks, Sarah increased the time of her walks and added a few bodyweight exercises. Eventually, she was working out for 45 minutes each day and had lost the 50 pounds she had once thought impossible. By focusing on small wins, Sarah built the consistency and momentum necessary to reach her larger goal.

2. Tom's Career Transformation

Tom had spent years in a job he disliked, feeling stuck and unfulfilled. He knew he wanted to transition to a new career, but the thought of starting over in a completely new field was daunting. Instead of diving straight into the deep end,

Tom started by setting a small, manageable goal: he would dedicate just 15 minutes every morning to researching his desired field. Each day, he would read articles, listen to podcasts, and watch videos to learn more about the industry. At first, 15 minutes felt trivial, but over time, it became a habit, and he gained enough knowledge and confidence to take the next step. A few months later, Tom enrolled in an online course, then began networking with others in the industry. Eventually, Tom made a successful career switch, all by leveraging the power of small wins to build momentum.

3. Maria's Writing Goals

Maria dreamed of writing a book but was paralyzed by the idea of sitting down to write an entire manuscript. She had tried several times to write, but the task always felt too big. She knew she had a message to share but couldn't find the motivation to start. So, Maria decided to take a different approach. She committed to writing just 200 words a day—nothing more, nothing less. The goal was so small that it felt easy to accomplish. At first, it didn't seem like much, but over time, the habit took hold. After a few weeks, she found herself writing more than the 200 words she had set as a goal. Eventually, Maria finished the manuscript, all because she started small and built momentum with daily wins.

The Power of Small Wins in Daily Life

Small wins can be applied to any area of life, from personal goals to professional development, health, relationships, and beyond. The beauty of this approach is that you don't have to wait for the perfect moment or the grand gesture to start moving forward. You can begin right now, with something small. Whether it's making your bed in the morning, sending one email, reading a few pages of a book, or meditating for five minutes, the key is to begin, no matter how small the task seems. Over time, you'll look back and realize how far you've come, all thanks to the accumulation of small wins.

By embracing the power of small wins, you can break free from the inertia that holds you back, overcome procrastination, and build momentum that propels you toward your dreams. The path to overcoming laziness isn't about taking giant leaps—it's about making steady progress, one small step at a time. Remember, success isn't about perfection; it's about consistency. And with every small win, you move one step closer to realizing your full potential.

◊ ◊ ◊ ◊

Chapter 5:

Rule 5: Overcome Procrastination

◊ ◊ ◊ ◊

Chapter 5: Rule 5 – Overcome Procrastination

Procrastination is often mistaken for laziness, but they are not the same. While laziness is characterized by a lack of desire to act, procrastination is more insidious—a deliberate delay of action despite knowing its importance. If laziness is sitting idly, procrastination is busying yourself with unimportant tasks to avoid confronting what truly matters. They are cousins, sharing similar traits but operating in different ways, both capable of halting progress and burying potential under the weight of inaction. To overcome laziness, it's imperative to address procrastination head-on, understand its triggers, and cultivate habits that propel you into action.

Procrastination: The Silent Saboteur

Procrastination often feels harmless in the moment. "I'll do it tomorrow," you tell yourself, believing there will be more time, more energy, or more inspiration waiting for you. Yet, tomorrow comes, and the same cycle repeats. Tasks pile up, deadlines loom closer, and the weight of inaction grows heavier. The consequence of procrastination isn't just missed opportunities—it's the erosion of self-confidence, a gnawing guilt that whispers you're capable of more but unwilling to act.

At its core, procrastination stems from fear: fear of failure, fear of discomfort, fear of imperfection. The brain, seeking to avoid stress or unpleasant emotions, opts for easier, more pleasurable activities in the short term. You scroll through social media, reorganize your desk, or binge-watch a series—not because these tasks matter but because they distract you from what does. Overcoming procrastination isn't about forcing yourself into action with sheer willpower; it's about rewiring your relationship with time, tasks, and the fears that hold you back.

Identifying Triggers and Distractions

Before you can conquer procrastination, you must first understand it. What pulls you away from important tasks? Are you easily distracted by your phone, social media, or television? Do you avoid certain responsibilities because they feel overwhelming or boring? Identifying your procrastination triggers is like shining a light on an invisible enemy—it's the first step toward regaining control.

For many, procrastination begins with an environment ripe for distraction. A cluttered workspace invites interruptions. Notifications on your phone lure you into an endless loop of checking, liking, and scrolling. Even well-meaning friends or family can derail your focus. Recognizing these distractions and minimizing their influence is key to creating a space where productivity can thrive.

Sometimes, procrastination isn't about external distractions but internal resistance. Tasks that feel too big, too complicated, or too uncertain can trigger avoidance. The thought of starting a major project, for instance, might seem so daunting that you put it off, hoping for a mythical future where you'll magically feel ready. Understanding why you resist certain tasks—whether it's fear of failure or perfectionism—can help you develop strategies to overcome them.

Tools and Techniques to Combat Procrastination

Overcoming procrastination doesn't require a complete personality overhaul; it requires practical tools and techniques that make action easier. By implementing strategies designed to break tasks into manageable chunks and foster focus, you can transform procrastination into productivity.

The Pomodoro Technique

The Pomodoro Technique is a simple, yet powerful time-management method designed to combat procrastination by breaking work into focused intervals, typically 25 minutes long, followed by a short break. Named after a tomato-shaped kitchen timer, this technique works because it creates a sense of urgency and structure. Instead of staring at a mountain of work, you commit to just 25 minutes of focused effort.

When using the Pomodoro Technique, you set a timer and immerse yourself in your task for the designated interval. During this time, distractions are off-limits—no checking your phone, no replying to emails, no wandering into the kitchen for a snack. Once the timer rings, you take a 5-minute break to recharge before starting the next interval. After completing four intervals, you reward yourself with a longer break.

This method is effective because it transforms procrastination-prone tasks into bite-sized, approachable sessions. It also builds momentum: once you complete the first interval, you're more likely to continue working, riding the wave of progress.

Time-Blocking

Time-blocking is another powerful technique that helps you reclaim control over your schedule and combat procrastination. By assigning specific tasks to predetermined time slots, you eliminate the uncertainty of "when" you'll tackle your responsibilities. Instead of saying, "I'll work on this later," you decide in advance: "From 10:00 AM to 11:00 AM, I'll write the report."

This method forces you to confront your priorities and allocate time to what truly matters. It also prevents tasks from expanding endlessly, as you work within the boundaries of the designated time slot. When you time-block effectively, procrastination loses its grip because there's no ambiguity—your schedule is a roadmap guiding you toward productivity.

The 2-Minute Rule

One of the simplest and most effective strategies for overcoming procrastination is the 2-Minute Rule. The premise is straightforward: if a task will take less than two minutes to complete, do it immediately. Respond to that email, wash that dish, or make that quick phone call instead of letting it linger on your to-do list.

For larger tasks, the 2-Minute Rule can be adapted to help you get started. Commit to working on a daunting task for just two minutes. The goal isn't to finish it—it's to break through the initial barrier of inaction. More often than not, once you start, you'll find it easier to keep going. Action begets action, and the simple act of beginning can dissolve the mental resistance that fuels procrastination.

The "Eat the Frog" Technique

The "Eat the Frog" technique, popularized by Brian Tracy, is a powerful method for overcoming procrastination by tackling your most challenging or important task first thing in the day. The name comes from the idea that if you had to eat a live frog every morning, the rest of the day would seem easy in comparison. In this metaphor, your "frog" represents the task you're most likely to procrastinate on but also the one that will have the greatest positive impact if completed.

By starting your day with this priority task, you accomplish something significant right away, setting a productive tone for the rest of your day. This method works because it eliminates the mental burden of carrying the task forward, freeing up energy and focus for other responsibilities.

To implement this technique:

Identify Your Frog:

At the end of each day, review your to-do list and highlight the one task that is most important or the one you've been avoiding.

Commit to Eating It First:

Before diving into emails, social media, or easier tasks, dedicate the first part of your day to this priority.

Minimize Distractions:

Create a focused environment to tackle the task without interruptions.

Reward Yourself:

Celebrate your accomplishment with a small reward, such as a short break, a favourite snack, or an activity you enjoy.

The "Eat the Frog" technique is highly effective because it addresses procrastination head-on, helping you build momentum and confidence as you complete high-value tasks. By consistently applying this approach, you'll develop a habit of prioritizing what matters most and taking decisive action, even when the task feels daunting.

Building a Procrastination-Proof Routine

Overcoming procrastination isn't a one-time fix; it's a lifestyle shift. To make lasting changes, you need to build routines and habits that prioritize action and minimize avoidance. Begin each day by identifying your top priorities—the tasks that matter most—and tackle them during your peak productivity hours.

Create an environment that supports focus. Eliminate distractions by turning off notifications, decluttering your workspace, and setting boundaries with those around you. Use tools like the Pomodoro Technique or time-blocking to structure your day and ensure that important tasks are completed without delay.

Celebrate your progress, no matter how small. Each time you resist the urge to procrastinate and take meaningful action, you're strengthening your ability to overcome it in the future. Acknowledge these victories and remind yourself of the greater purpose behind your efforts.

Real-Life Transformations

Procrastination may feel like an insurmountable obstacle, but countless people have proven that it can be conquered. Once again, the names of these people, of course, are pseudonyms. Take John, for example, a freelance designer who struggled to meet deadlines because he constantly delayed starting his projects. By implementing the Pomodoro Technique, John found that he could break his work into manageable intervals, making the process less overwhelming. Over time, he not only met his deadlines but also exceeded client expectations.

Or consider Emma, a college student who found herself overwhelmed by the sheer volume of assignments. By using time-blocking, Emma allocated specific hours to each subject and stuck to her schedule. This approach not only improved her grades but also reduced her stress levels, as she no longer felt the weight of unfinished tasks hanging over her.

These stories serve as a reminder that procrastination is not a permanent state. With the right strategies and mindset, anyone can break free from its grip and achieve their goals.

Moving Forward

Procrastination may be the cousin of laziness, but it doesn't have to be your companion. By understanding its triggers, using practical tools like the Pomodoro Technique and the 2-Minute Rule, and creating a routine that prioritizes action, you can reclaim control over your time and your life.

The journey to overcome procrastination begins with a single step—a step away from avoidance and toward action. Start small, stay consistent, and remember that progress, not perfection, is the goal. Every task you complete, every moment of focus, and every decision to act brings you closer to the life you envision.

◊ ◊ ◊ ◊

Chapter 6:
Rule 6: Optimize Your Environment

◊ ◊ ◊ ◊

Chapter 6: Rule 6 – Optimize Your Environment

Our environment wields incredible power over us, often in ways we don't realize. Just as a seed needs the right soil to grow, your productivity and drive thrive when you cultivate the right surroundings. The cluttered desk, the incessant buzz of notifications, or even the subtle chaos of a poorly arranged room can sap your energy and steer you toward laziness. By intentionally shaping your environment to support focus and productivity, you can transform your daily experience and break free from the grip of inaction.

The Invisible Influence of Your Environment

Have you ever noticed how walking into a serene, well-organized space can immediately put your mind at ease, while a messy or chaotic one leaves you feeling frazzled and unmotivated? This isn't just a coincidence. Your surroundings have a profound psychological impact on your ability to focus, your mood, and even your willingness to take action.

Imagine trying to work on an important project while your desk is piled high with papers, your phone is lighting up with notifications, and the television hums in the background. It's like trying to sprint through a swamp—you'll make some progress, but it will be slow, exhausting, and far from your best effort. Conversely, a clean, orderly environment with minimal distractions acts like a clear, open path, making it easier to focus and gain momentum.

Your environment doesn't just passively influence you; it actively shapes your habits. If laziness has been a recurring theme in your life, take a closer look at the spaces you inhabit. Are they designed to encourage action, or do they enable procrastination? The good news is that you have the power to take control and optimize your environment to work for you, not against you.

Declutter to Declutter Your Mind

Physical clutter is more than just an eyesore—it's a source of mental noise. Each time you glance at that pile of papers, the unwashed dishes, or the overflowing inbox, you're reminded of unfinished tasks and unmet expectations. Over time, this visual chaos can contribute to a sense of overwhelm, making it harder to start anything new.

Decluttering your physical space isn't just about tidying up; it's about creating an atmosphere of clarity and possibility. Start with your immediate work or living area. Clear off your desk, organize your tools, and find designated places for your belongings. When your space is orderly, your mind feels lighter, and the path to action becomes more visible.

Digital clutter is equally insidious. A desktop full of random files, an inbox with thousands of unread emails, or a phone overloaded with apps and notifications can drain your focus. Take time to organize your digital spaces: sort files into folders, unsubscribe from unnecessary email lists, and delete apps that no longer serve you. Every bit of decluttering reduces friction and frees up mental energy to focus on what truly matters.

The Power of a Distraction-Free Zone

In today's hyperconnected world, distractions are everywhere. Your phone buzzes with notifications, your browser tempts you with endless tabs, and even well-meaning friends or family can interrupt your flow. If you want to overcome laziness and cultivate sustained focus, creating a distraction-free zone is non-negotiable.

A distraction-free zone isn't about building a fortress of solitude; it's about intentionally designing a space that supports your goals. Start by identifying a specific area where you can work, study, or pursue personal projects without interruptions. This could be a corner of your home, a desk at the library, or even a quiet café. The key is consistency—use this space exclusively for focused activities, so your mind associates it with productivity.

Eliminate as many potential distractions as possible. Turn off unnecessary notifications on your phone and computer, invest in noise-cancelling headphones if needed, and communicate boundaries to those around you. Let your family or roommates know when you need uninterrupted time and consider using tools like a "do not disturb" sign or a time-blocking schedule to reinforce your focus.

Distractions aren't always external; internal distractions, like wandering thoughts or the urge to procrastinate, can be just as disruptive. Combat these by grounding yourself in the present moment. Techniques like mindfulness, deep breathing, or setting a clear intention for your work session can help you stay centred and engaged.

Real-Life Transformations

Here are some real-life transformations of those who optimized their surroundings. These are, once again, their pseudonyms.

Consider the story of Lily, a graphic designer who struggled to meet deadlines because her workspace was perpetually chaotic. Her desk was cluttered with old sketches, half-empty coffee cups, and random knickknacks. Her computer desktop was no better—files were scattered everywhere, and she spent more time searching for assets than creating.

One weekend, Lily decided to tackle the chaos. She spent a day decluttering her desk, organizing her tools, and creating a system for her digital files. She also set up a small corkboard with inspiring images and quotes to keep her motivated. The difference was night and day. With her workspace in order, Lily found it easier to focus, her creativity flourished, and she consistently delivered projects ahead of schedule.

Then there's Marcus, a college student who found himself constantly distracted by his phone while studying. He created a distraction-free zone by designating a specific spot in his home for studying and leaving his phone in another room during study sessions. He also started using a simple timer to track his focus. These small changes led to dramatic improvements in his grades and overall confidence.

Designing an Environment for Success

Optimizing your environment isn't a one-time event; it's an ongoing process of refinement. Start small and build from there. Begin by decluttering a single area, such as your desk or your digital workspace. Once you experience the benefits of a clear, distraction-free zone, expand the principles to other areas of your life.

Surround yourself with cues that inspire action. Place motivational quotes, vision boards, or reminders of your goals in your workspace. Keep the tools you need within easy reach, so there's no excuse to delay starting a task. Conversely, remove or hide items that tempt you to procrastinate, like your gaming console, junk food, or social media apps.

Remember, your environment is a reflection of your priorities. If you value focus, growth, and achievement, let your surroundings reflect that. Take pride in creating spaces that empower you to show up as your best self every day.

Moving Forward

Your environment is more than just a backdrop; it's a powerful force that can either propel you forward or hold you back. By optimizing your surroundings to minimize distractions, reduce clutter, and support focus, you create the ideal conditions for productivity and growth.

The journey to overcoming laziness doesn't require dramatic changes overnight. Start with simple steps—declutter one space, silence one distraction, or designate one area for focused work. Each small improvement adds up, building momentum and reinforcing your commitment to a more purposeful life.

Take charge of your environment today. Transform it into a space that energizes you, inspires you, and makes taking action the easiest choice. You don't have to be perfect; you just have to begin.

◊ ◊ ◊ ◊

Chapter 7:

Rule 7 – Energy Management

◊ ◊ ◊ ◊

Chapter 7: Rule 7 – Energy Management

Energy is the silent driver of every action we take. Without it, even the simplest tasks feel insurmountable, and laziness becomes the default. But when your energy is vibrant and well-managed, you feel unstoppable, capable of tackling challenges head-on. Energy isn't just physical; it's mental, emotional, and spiritual. Managing it effectively is one of the most empowering ways to overcome laziness and maintain productivity.

The Connection Between Energy and Laziness

At its core, laziness often stems from low energy. Have you ever had a day where even though you wanted to accomplish something, your body felt heavy and your mind foggy? This isn't a lack of ambition—it's a sign that your energy reserves are depleted.

Laziness thrives in an environment of exhaustion and imbalance. It's easy to label yourself as unmotivated when, in reality, your body and mind simply need replenishment. By learning to manage your energy effectively, you remove one of the biggest barriers to action and unlock the stamina to pursue your goals.

The good news? Energy management is a skill you can cultivate. It doesn't require superhuman effort—just a series of small, consistent choices that prioritize your well-being and vitality.

Prioritize Sleep: The Foundation of Energy

Sleep is the cornerstone of energy management. It's during those precious hours of rest that your body repairs itself, your mind processes information, and your spirit is recharged. Yet, in a culture that glorifies hustle, sleep is often the first thing sacrificed.

When you skimp on sleep, your productivity, mood, and focus take a hit. Laziness becomes a tempting escape because your body lacks the fuel to power through the day. Conversely, when you prioritize quality sleep, you wake up refreshed, alert, and ready to take on the world.

Start by creating a consistent bedtime routine. Treat sleep as sacred—dim the lights, turn off screens at least an hour before bed, and engage in calming activities like reading or meditation. Aim for 7–8 hours of uninterrupted rest each night. Over time, you'll notice the profound impact that good sleep has on your energy levels and motivation.

Eat for Energy: Fuel Your Fire

Your body is a machine, and food is its fuel. The quality of what you eat determines the energy you'll have to conquer the day. Highly processed foods, sugary snacks, and caffeine overloads might give you a temporary boost, but they lead to energy crashes that sap your momentum.

Instead, focus on balanced meals that provide sustained energy. Start your day with a breakfast that combines complex carbohydrates, healthy fats, and protein. Think oatmeal with fresh fruit and nuts or scrambled eggs with whole-grain toast. At lunch and dinner, prioritize lean proteins, whole grains, and plenty of vegetables.

Snacking is also a powerful tool. Instead of reaching for chips or candy, opt for nutrient-dense options like Greek yogurt with almonds, carrot sticks with hummus, or a banana with peanut butter. These foods keep your energy stable and help you avoid the dreaded afternoon slump.

Hydration is equally critical. Dehydration is a sneaky culprit behind fatigue. Keep a water bottle with you throughout the day and aim for at least eight glasses of water. Add a slice of lemon or a few mint leaves for flavour if plain water feels dull.

Move Your Body: Energize Your Spirit

It might seem counterintuitive, but movement is one of the best ways to combat low energy. Exercise doesn't drain your energy—it amplifies it by improving circulation, boosting endorphins, and enhancing your overall vitality.

You don't need to run marathons or spend hours in the gym. Even light, consistent movement can make a significant difference. Start your mornings with gentle stretches to wake up your muscles and increase flexibility. After meals, take a 10-minute walk to aid digestion and refresh your mind. During work breaks, try desk exercises like shoulder rolls, seated leg lifts, or simple neck stretches.

If your schedule allows, incorporate more structured exercise like yoga, cycling, or strength training into your routine. These activities not only build physical endurance but also sharpen your focus and elevate your mood.

Manage Energy Dips: Listen to Your Body

No matter how well you manage your energy, dips are inevitable. The key is to recognize them and respond strategically rather than pushing through with sheer willpower.

The afternoon slump, for example, is a common energy dip. Instead of reaching for another cup of coffee, try a light snack like a handful of trail mix or an apple with almond butter. Pair it with a quick walk or a few minutes of mindfulness to recharge.

Pay attention to what your body is telling you. If you're consistently tired at the same time each day, it might be a sign to adjust your schedule, incorporate more breaks, or reevaluate your diet.

Tools for Energy Management

Energy management isn't just about habits; it's about using tools and techniques that support your efforts. One effective method is the Pomodoro Technique, where you work in focused intervals (usually 25 minutes) followed by short breaks. This approach not only prevents burnout but also keeps your energy levels steady throughout the day.

Time-blocking is another powerful tool. By scheduling tasks during your peak energy hours, you can tackle demanding activities when you're at your best. Save less intensive tasks, like emails or organizing files, for times when your energy naturally wanes.

Caffeine can be a helpful ally when used strategically. Enjoy your morning coffee or tea but avoid consuming caffeine in the late afternoon or evening—it can interfere with your sleep and create a cycle of energy crashes.

Real-Life Transformations

Yet again, we have real-life transformations as evidence of successful energy management. Again, pseudonyms are used.

Consider Sarah, a busy entrepreneur who used to rely on endless cups of coffee and late-night work sessions to get through her days. Her energy was erratic, and she often felt overwhelmed. By prioritizing sleep, eating balanced meals, and incorporating a short morning workout, Sarah transformed her routine. She now has steady energy, greater focus, and more time for her personal life.

Or take James, a student who struggled to stay awake during lectures and procrastinated on assignments. Once he started using the Pomodoro Technique and taking afternoon walks, his energy levels stabilized. He found it easier to focus and complete tasks on time, leaving room for relaxation and hobbies.

Closing Thoughts

Energy management is about treating yourself as a priority. It's about recognizing that your well-being isn't an obstacle to productivity—it's the foundation of it. By getting enough sleep, eating nourishing foods, moving your body, and respecting your natural rhythms, you equip yourself with the vitality to overcome laziness and achieve your goals.

Remember, energy is finite but renewable. Each small choice you make—whether it's drinking a glass of water, stepping outside for fresh air, or going to bed on time—adds up to a life filled with momentum and purpose. You deserve to feel energized and capable every day, so start making those choices today. Let energy be the force that propels you toward the life you want to create.

◊ ◊ ◊ ◊

Chapter 8:

Rule 8 – Accountability and Support Systems

◊ ◊ ◊ ◊

Chapter 8: Rule 8 – Accountability and Support Systems

Overcoming laziness is not a journey you need to take alone. While personal determination is critical, the presence of others in your corner can amplify your progress, provide encouragement during setbacks, and serve as a beacon of motivation when your inner drive falters. Accountability and support systems are like the wind beneath your wings—quiet yet powerful forces that help you soar higher than you ever could on your own.

Why Accountability Matters

Imagine this: you've set a goal to wake up at 6 a.m. every day and go for a jog. On the first day, your alarm goes off, and you muster the energy to rise. But by day three, the warmth of your bed feels irresistible. You hit snooze, promising yourself that tomorrow you'll get up. Tomorrow becomes next week, and before long, the goal slips away entirely.

Now, picture the same scenario, but this time, a friend is waiting for you at the park, ready to jog with you. Suddenly, skipping feels less like a tempting option and more like letting someone down. That subtle shift—the knowledge that someone else is counting on you—can make all the difference.

Accountability isn't just about external pressure; it's about commitment. When you know someone is checking in on your progress, you become more invested in your goals. You feel a heightened sense of responsibility—not just to them, but to yourself. This creates a positive feedback loop where consistent action builds confidence, and confidence fuels further action.

Building a Supportive Community

One of the most transformative steps you can take in overcoming laziness is surrounding yourself with people who uplift, inspire, and challenge you. A supportive community serves as a constant reminder that you're not alone in your journey and that your efforts matter.

Start by identifying an accountability partner. This person doesn't need to share the exact same goals as you, but they should understand the value of discipline and growth. It could be a friend who's working on their own self-improvement journey, a family member who's willing to support you, or even a colleague who shares professional ambitions. Schedule regular check-ins—these can be as simple as a weekly phone call or a shared progress chart.

If one-on-one accountability feels limiting, consider joining a group. Whether it's a local fitness class, a book club, or a professional networking circle, groups provide a sense of camaraderie and shared purpose. Being surrounded by like-minded individuals creates an environment where progress feels contagious. You'll find yourself inspired by others' achievements and encouraged to share your own.

For those who thrive in digital spaces, online communities offer endless possibilities. Platforms like Reddit, Facebook Groups, and Discord host vibrant forums for nearly every interest and goal imaginable. Engage with these communities not just as a passive observer, but as an active participant. Share your struggles, celebrate your wins, and offer support to others. The more you invest in these interactions, the more you'll reap the rewards of collective motivation.

Tools and Apps for Accountability

In the age of technology, there's no shortage of tools designed to keep you on track. These apps and platforms serve as virtual coaches, offering reminders, tracking progress, and even gamifying the process of self-improvement.

Habit-tracking apps like Habitica, Streaks, and Done transform your goals into actionable, trackable habits. They allow you to set daily tasks, monitor your streaks, and receive rewarding visuals that celebrate your consistency.

If you thrive on real-time interaction, accountability platforms like Focusmate provide a unique solution. Focusmate pairs you with a virtual partner for live co-working sessions, ensuring you stay focused and productive during set time blocks.

For goal-setting enthusiasts, tools like Trello and Asana offer structured ways to break tasks into smaller steps, set deadlines, and visualize your progress. These platforms not only keep you organized but also make your goals feel tangible and achievable.

Daily journaling apps like Daylio or Reflectly encourages self-reflection. By documenting your thoughts, feelings, and accomplishments, you gain deeper insight into your patterns and triggers. Journaling serves as a private accountability tool, helping you track progress and stay aligned with your intentions.

Maintaining Motivation in Your Community

Building a support system is just the beginning. The real magic happens when you actively nurture these connections, ensuring they remain sources of motivation and positivity.

One powerful way to do this is by celebrating wins together. Achieving a goal, no matter how small, is an accomplishment worth acknowledging. Whether it's a simple congratulatory text, a shared meal, or a virtual high-five, these celebrations create a sense of progress and pride that fuels further efforts.

Transparency is equally important. Laziness often thrives in secrecy; when you hide your struggles, they gain power over you. By openly discussing challenges with your accountability partner or community, you create space for support and solutions. Vulnerability builds trust, and trust fosters growth.

Consider setting group goals to foster a sense of shared purpose. For example, you and your accountability partner might commit to a 30-day fitness challenge, or your online community might organize a virtual study session. Collaborating on goals strengthens bonds and amplifies motivation.

Real-Life Transformations Through Accountability

Once again, pseudonyms are used in this section to provide confidentiality.

Think about Emma, a writer who struggled with procrastination for years. She joined an online writing group and committed to submitting one short story per month. The group's feedback, encouragement, and shared deadlines transformed her approach. Within a year, Emma completed a novel—a dream she'd previously thought impossible.

Then there's David, a software developer who felt stuck in his career. He partnered with a colleague to set weekly professional goals, such as learning a new programming language or attending a webinar. Their mutual accountability not only boosted their skills but also deepened their friendship.

These stories illustrate a universal truth: when you align your goals with the power of community, the journey becomes less daunting and far more rewarding.

Moving Forward Together

The journey to overcoming laziness is not meant to be a solitary one. Accountability and support systems remind you that your goals matter—not just to you, but to those who care about your growth. They provide a safety net for when you stumble and a cheerleading squad for when you succeed.

Take the first step today. Reach out to someone who inspires you, join a group that aligns with your interests, or explore tools that resonate with your style. The effort you invest in building these connections will repay you tenfold, not just in progress but in the joy of shared experiences.

Remember, the path to self-discipline and productivity isn't a lonely road. It's a communal journey filled with encouragement, inspiration, and support. When you walk alongside others, you'll find that every step becomes lighter, and every goal feels within reach. Let accountability and support be the pillars that elevate you to new heights—because you don't have to do it alone.

◊ ◊ ◊ ◊

Chapter 9:

Rule 9 – Embrace Discipline Over Motivation

◊ ◊ ◊ ◊

Chapter 9: Rule 9 – Embrace Discipline Over Motivation

Motivation is like a shooting star. It blazes through the sky, momentarily capturing our attention and inspiring awe, but it doesn't last. Discipline, however, is the steady lighthouse, unwavering in its presence, guiding ships through stormy seas and calm waters alike. If overcoming laziness is your goal, then discipline, not motivation, is the tool you need to master.

We often fall into the trap of waiting for motivation to strike, believing that inspiration is the spark we need to take action. But the truth is, motivation is unreliable. It waxes and wanes with our emotions, external circumstances, and fleeting moments of enthusiasm. Discipline, on the other hand, is a deliberate choice—a commitment to show up, regardless of how you feel. It's not flashy or glamorous, but it is powerful. Discipline sustains the effort needed to achieve greatness, long after motivation fades.

The Power of Discipline: Real-Life Stories

History is filled with individuals who didn't rely on motivation but instead leaned into the power of discipline to achieve their dreams.

Take **J.K. Rowling**, for example. Long before she became a literary icon, Rowling faced rejection after rejection. A single mother living on government assistance, her days were filled with challenges. Motivation alone could not have carried her through; it was her discipline—the choice to sit down and write every day—that brought the magical world of Harry Potter to life. She didn't wait for the perfect mood or conditions. She committed to her craft, and that unwavering discipline turned her vision into a phenomenon that touched millions.

Or consider **David Goggins**, who has been dubbed "the toughest man alive." Once an overweight exterminator with a life he wasn't proud of, Goggins decided to rewrite his story. He didn't rely on fleeting bursts of motivation to propel him forward. Instead, he built a disciplined routine, tackling daily actions that pushed him closer to his goals. Over time, he transformed into a Navy SEAL, an ultramarathon runner, and a beacon of mental toughness. His story is a testament to the fact that small, consistent actions, driven by discipline, can break even the most formidable barriers.

Then there's **Serena Williams**, one of the greatest athletes in history. Her unparalleled success in tennis isn't a result of sporadic bursts of inspiration but of years of disciplined training, mental fortitude, and relentless effort. Even on days when she didn't feel like hitting the court, she showed up. Her discipline created a legacy that will inspire generations.

These stories illustrate that discipline, not motivation, is the backbone of achievement. It is the unshakable force that carries individuals through adversity, doubt, and monotony toward their dreams.

Why Discipline Trumps Motivation

Motivation, for all its appeal, is fleeting. It can spark action but rarely sustains it. One day, you wake up brimming with excitement about a new goal; the next, you're tempted to stay in bed. Discipline, however, is consistent. It doesn't depend on how you feel or whether circumstances are ideal. It's the decision to act, day after day, regardless of external factors.

When you rely solely on motivation, you're at the mercy of your emotions. If you're tired, stressed, or uninspired, your progress stalls. Discipline, on the other hand, creates momentum. Each disciplined action builds on the last, forming habits that eventually operate on autopilot. Over time, the effort required to maintain discipline decreases, but the rewards compound exponentially.

Discipline is what gets you out of bed on a cold morning when motivation whispers that you deserve another hour of sleep. It's what keeps you working on your goals when setbacks arise, or progress feels slow. It's the bridge between dreams and reality, ensuring that your efforts are consistent, even when inspiration falters.

Building Discipline: A Structured Approach

Developing discipline is a skill, not an innate trait. Anyone can cultivate it with the right strategies and a commitment to practice.

Start small. Discipline doesn't require monumental leaps; it thrives on small, manageable actions. For instance, if you want to exercise regularly, start with just 10 minutes a day. This small win builds confidence and establishes a routine that you can expand over time.

Creating routines is another cornerstone of discipline. When you establish a daily schedule, you reduce decision fatigue and make it easier to stay on track. Block off specific times for activities that align with your goals, whether it's exercising, studying, or working on a passion project. The more consistent your routine, the less effort it takes to maintain discipline.

Eliminate distractions that threaten to derail your focus. This could mean using website blockers, silencing your phone during work sessions, or creating a dedicated workspace free from interruptions. Discipline thrives in environments that support focus and minimize temptation.

Embrace discomfort. Growth often requires stepping outside your comfort zone and tackling tasks that feel challenging or tedious. Discipline is built when you choose to act, even when it's hard. For example, if you're procrastinating on a task, commit to just five minutes of work. Often, taking the first step reduces resistance and propels you forward.

Track your progress to reinforce your efforts. Whether you use a journal, an app, or a simple checklist, documenting your actions provides tangible evidence of your growth. This visual reminder of your discipline can be incredibly motivating, especially on days when progress feels slow.

Finally, reward consistency. Celebrate the small wins that come from disciplined action. These rewards don't have to be extravagant—a favourite treat, a relaxing evening, or a personal acknowledgment can reinforce your commitment and make the process more enjoyable.

Reflection: Discipline in Your Own Life

Think back to a time when you accomplished something meaningful. What role did discipline play in your success? Perhaps it was sticking to a study schedule that helped you ace an exam, committing to daily practice that improved your skills, or persisting through challenges to achieve a personal milestone.

Remember how it felt to push through obstacles and achieve your goal. That sense of pride and fulfilment is the reward of discipline.

Discipline isn't about perfection; it's about persistence. It's the choice to keep moving forward, even when the path is steep, or the journey feels long. Every time you practice discipline, you strengthen your ability to act with intention and align your actions with your values.

Moving Forward with This Mindset

Motivation may light the spark, but discipline keeps the fire burning. It's the steadfast companion that ensures you continue to make progress, even when enthusiasm wanes. By embracing discipline, you equip yourself with a tool that transcends fleeting emotions and external circumstances.

Start small, create routines, eliminate distractions, and embrace discomfort. Each act of discipline is a step closer to the life you envision—a life defined not by fleeting inspiration but by deliberate, consistent action. Let discipline be the engine that drives you forward, and you'll find that success is not only possible but inevitable.

In the words of Aristotle, "We are what we repeatedly do. Excellence, then, is not an act, but a habit." Discipline is the key to forming those habits, unlocking your potential, and achieving the extraordinary. So don't wait for motivation to strike. Choose discipline and take the first step today.

◊ ◊ ◊ ◊

Chapter 10:

Rule 10 – Embrace Discipline Over Motivation

◊ ◊ ◊ ◊

Chapter 10: Rule 10 – Reward Yourself and Celebrate Progress

We are back again at emphasizing rewarding ourselves. Life is a journey, not just a destination. When working to overcome laziness and embrace productivity, one of the most important steps is learning to celebrate progress—no matter how small. Rewards are not just indulgences; they're fuel that keeps your motivation alive and your spirit energized. By acknowledging your achievements and taking time to reflect on your growth, you create a positive feedback loop that propels you forward toward even greater accomplishments.

The Joy of Celebrating Wins

Too often, we focus on what's left to do, overlooking how far we've already come. This mindset can sap our energy, making us feel as though we're constantly climbing an insurmountable mountain. But when you pause to celebrate your victories—whether it's finishing a challenging project, sticking to a new habit for a week, or simply taking the first step—you're reminding yourself that you are capable, determined, and deserving of pride.

Celebrating wins, both big and small, isn't just about feeling good in the moment. It's about reinforcing the habits and behaviours that brought you success in the first place. Every celebration act as a psychological reward, signalling to your brain that the effort you put in was worthwhile. This positive reinforcement strengthens your resolve, making it easier to stay consistent even when the going gets tough.

The Art of Rewarding Yourself

Building a reward system is more than just a strategy—it's an art form. The key is to align your rewards with your goals and values, ensuring that they genuinely feel like a treat rather than an afterthought. A well-designed reward system can transform even the most mundane tasks into something you look forward to.

Start by identifying what truly brings you joy. Maybe it's taking a relaxing bubble bath, indulging in your favourite meal, binge-watching a show guilt-free, or buying yourself a small gift. The reward doesn't have to be extravagant—it just needs to resonate with you.

For example, if your goal is to exercise regularly, reward yourself with a new playlist or workout gear after completing a month of consistent sessions. If you're working on a big project, treat yourself to a day off or a fun outing once it's done. Tying rewards to milestones gives you something tangible to look forward to, turning the act of hard work into a game you want to win.

Celebrating Small Wins: A Key to Momentum

Big achievements may take weeks, months, or even years to accomplish. Waiting for those moments to celebrate can leave you feeling drained and unmotivated along the way. That's why it's crucial to celebrate small wins, the little steps that inch you closer to your goal.

Did you complete a challenging task today? Reward yourself with a short break or a favourite snack. Did you resist procrastination and start something you've been avoiding? Give yourself a pat on the back and acknowledge the effort it took to overcome inertia. Each small celebration adds a spark to your journey, turning daily efforts into moments of joy.

Real progress is built on consistency, and small wins keep the momentum alive. Over time, these victories compound, leading to bigger and more significant achievements.

Reflection as a Celebration

Celebration isn't always about external rewards. Sometimes, the most powerful form of recognition comes from within. Reflection is a way to celebrate progress on a deeper level, allowing you to connect with your growth and learn from your experiences.

Set aside time to look back on what you've achieved. Write about it in a journal, create a vision board showcasing your milestones, or simply spend a quiet moment thinking about how far you've come. Ask yourself:

"What were the biggest challenges I faced, and how did I overcome them?"

"What habits or strategies worked best for me?"

"What am I most proud of?"

By reflecting on these questions, you gain insight into your journey, reinforcing the lessons that have helped you grow. Reflection also helps you identify areas for improvement, ensuring that your future efforts are even more effective.

Building a Celebration Ritual

To make celebrating progress a consistent part of your life, consider creating a ritual. This could be as simple as lighting a candle and taking a moment to meditate on your achievements, or as elaborate as hosting a monthly "victory dinner" where you toast to your successes.

Having a ritual gives you something to look forward to, turning the act of celebration into a cherished tradition. It also signals to your subconscious that your efforts are valuable, worthy of recognition, and deserving of joy.

The Ripple Effect of Celebration

When you celebrate your progress, you're not just uplifting yourself—you're inspiring others around you. Sharing your wins with friends, family, or your community creates a ripple effect of positivity. It reminds others that hard work pays off, that progress is worth celebrating, and that they, too, can achieve their goals.

For example, if you're part of a group working toward similar objectives, celebrating as a team fosters camaraderie and mutual encouragement. Acknowledging each other's wins strengthens the bonds of support, making the journey less lonely and more rewarding for everyone involved.

Turning Setbacks into Opportunities

Even setbacks can be a cause for celebration—if you view them as opportunities to learn and grow. Instead of dwelling on what went wrong, take a moment to appreciate the lessons hidden within the challenges. Celebrate the fact that you had the courage to try and use the experience as fuel to move forward with greater wisdom and resilience.

Progress Over Perfection

One of the most important lessons in celebrating progress is understanding that perfection is not the goal—progress is. Celebrate the effort you put in, the strides you've made, and the determination that keeps you moving forward. Every step count, and every bit of progress is a victory worth acknowledging.

The Transformative Power of Celebration

At its heart, celebrating progress is about gratitude—for your efforts, your growth, and the journey you're on. It's about shifting your focus from what's lacking to what's abundant, from what you haven't done to what you've accomplished. This shift in perspective can be profoundly transformative, filling you with renewed energy, confidence, and a sense of purpose.

When you reward yourself and celebrate your wins, you're not just marking the end of a task—you're reinforcing the mindset and habits that will carry you through the next challenge. You're telling yourself, "I am capable, I am resilient, and I am worthy of success."

So go ahead. Celebrate boldly, reward yourself generously, and savour every step of your journey. The path to overcoming laziness and unlocking your potential is a long one, but with every win—big or small—you're proving to yourself that it's a journey worth taking.

◊ ◊ ◊ ◊

Conclusion:
Living Fully

◊ ◊ ◊ ◊

Conclusion: Living Fully

Laziness does not define you. Your choices, your actions, and the effort you put into living fully—that's what shapes your destiny. You hold the power to rewrite your story, one decision at a time. The journey you've embarked upon by exploring these ten rules is not just about overcoming laziness: it's about creating a life of purpose, passion, and possibility.

Each of these rules is a stepping stone toward a more vibrant and productive you. Rule 1 reminded us to know our "why", the unshakable reason behind our goals. This is your anchor, the guiding light that keeps you steady when the waves of doubt and distraction try to pull you under. Rule 2 taught us the art of setting clear goals and breaking them down into manageable steps. Big dreams become achievable when you focus on the small, consistent actions that bring them to life.

Rule 3 delved into mastering your mindset, where the battle against laziness truly begins. Negative self-talk and limiting beliefs lose their power when you cultivate positivity and resilience. Rule 4 emphasized the power of small wins—those little victories that create momentum and build confidence. Progress, no matter how modest, fuels a forward motion that's impossible to stop.

When procrastination strikes, Rule 5 provides the tools to overcome it. Techniques like the Pomodoro Technique, the "2-Minute Rule," and strategic time-blocking remind us that action, however small, is the antidote to inertia. And to sustain our energy for the long haul, Rule 6 and Rule 7 urge us to optimize our environment and manage our energy. Surroundings that inspire and habits that energize keep us focused, sharp, and ready to take on the world.

The role of others in our journey was highlighted in Rule 8, which emphasized accountability and support systems. The path to growth is never walked alone, and the encouragement of like-minded individuals can make all the difference. Rule 9 reminded us that discipline outlasts motivation. When inspiration fades, discipline steps in, guiding us to show up for ourselves even when we don't feel like it. And finally, Rule 10 celebrated the importance of rewarding yourself and reflecting on progress. Acknowledging your wins, both big and small, reinforces your efforts and keeps you inspired to reach even higher.

Together, these ten rules form a powerful roadmap to help you break free from the grip of laziness and step into a life brimming with potential. They are more than strategies—they are a mindset, a commitment to yourself to live fully and authentically.

But knowledge alone is not enough. Reading these pages is only the beginning. Transformation happens when you take action. It begins with a single step, however small. Maybe it's setting a single goal today, or decluttering your workspace, or reaching out to someone who can hold you accountable. What matters is that you start. The smallest step in the direction of your dreams carries more weight than the grandest intentions left unrealized.

As you move forward, remember that setbacks are part of the process. There will be days when the pull of laziness feels stronger, when the mountain seems too steep to climb. In those moments, return to your "why." Remind yourself that progress, not perfection, is the goal. Celebrate the effort, no matter how small, and keep going.

You are capable of more than you realize. The fact that you've come this far, that you've committed to learning and growing, is proof of your potential. Laziness may have held you back in the past, but it does not have to define your future. Every action you take in the direction of your goals is a declaration of your determination to live fully and purposefully.

Let's end with this empowering thought: The future belongs to those who take control of the present. What you do today shapes the life you will live tomorrow. Choose action. Choose growth. Choose to rise above the voice that says, "not now" and embrace the one that says, "I am ready."

As you close this book and step into the next chapter of your life, take with you this simple but powerful mantra: I am capable, I am disciplined, and I am worthy of success. Keep these words close and let them guide you as you create a life that is not only productive but deeply fulfilling.

The journey to overcoming laziness is the journey to becoming the best version of yourself. It's not always easy, but it is always worth it. So, take that first step, celebrate every stride, and never stop moving forward. Because you, my friend, are destined to live fully.

www.ingramcontent.com/pod-product-compliance
Lightning Source LLC
Chambersburg PA
CBHW070410230526
45471CB00006B/2737